Do Not Be Afraid, I Am With You

Do Not Be Afraid, I Am With You

Compiled and Edited by
Edmund C. Lane, SSP

ALBA · HOUSE   NEW · YORK
SOCIETY OF ST. PAUL, 2187 VICTORY BLVD., STATEN ISLAND, NY 10314

Produced and designed in the United States of
America by the Fathers and Brothers of the
Society of St. Paul, 2187 Victory Boulevard,
Staten Island, New York 10314, as part of their
communications apostolate.

ISBN: 0-8189-0617-0

Printing Information:

Current Printing - first digit	1	2	3	4	5	6	7	8	9	10	11	12
Year of Current Printing - first year shown					1991	1992	1993	1994	1995	1996	1997

Introduction

CONFINEMENT, A SPECIAL TIME TO PRAY

Our lives are albums written through
    With good or ill, with false or true;
And as the blessed angels turn
    The pages of our years,
God grant they read the good with smiles,
    And blot the ill with tears!
                        — *John Greenleaf Whittier*

There are circumstances and events in every life which wrench us out of our complacency and predictable routine and cause us to confront our weakness and mortality in a way that commands our full attention. An illness, an operation (indeed, confinement of any kind), our own or another's impending death, and the burial of a loved one all invite us to reflect on those things which truly matter and to turn our hearts to God in prayer.

The purpose of this little booklet is to help you through the difficulty that you presently encounter and to assist you in your efforts to examine, evaluate and reorient your life to God through prayer. May the compassionate presence of Jesus accompany you as you lift your mind to him in these pages. And may his words of encouragement — "Do not be afraid, I am with you!" — bring solace and comfort to your heart.

Prayer, as it has often been said, is a conversation with God. Hence, in compiling this book, we have tried to keep that fact in mind. In the Scripture readings we have let God speak; in the poetry and prayers, we have tried to present a springboard for your own reply.

Whatever the nature of your confinement — be it in a hospital bed, behind prison bars, or in the sanctuary of your own home — God is providing you at this time with a unique opportunity to draw closer to him and to grow in his grace. May the warmth of his love as manifested in all his works, comfort and strengthen you during this difficult period of your life. And may you find courage in the knowledge that the prayers of God's people accompany you all the way.

Rev. Edmund C. Lane, SSP
March 29, 1991
Good Friday

Contents

PART ONE: SCRIPTURE READINGS

1. GOD WISHES US TO HAVE LIFE

Wisdom 1:13-15

God did not make death, and he does not take pleasure in the death of the living. He has created everything so that they might exist. All creatures of the universe are wholesome and good... and the netherworld has no dominion over the earth, for righteousness is immortal.

Psalm 145:2-3, 4-5, 8-9, 10-11, 15-16, 21

R. (1) I will bless your name forever, Lord.

I will praise you day after day and exalt your name forever. Great is the Lord, most worthy of praise; his deeds are beyond all measure.

R. I will bless your name forever, Lord.

One generation shall commend your works to another and celebrate your acts of power. I will meditate on the splendor of your majesty and on the wondrous works which manifest your glory.

R. I will bless your name forever, Lord.

Compassionate and gracious is the Lord, slow to anger and abounding in love. The Lord is merciful to everyone; his love is for all his creation.

R. I will bless your name forever, Lord.

All your works will give you thanks, O Lord, and all your saints will praise you. They will tell of the glory of your kingdom, Lord, and speak of your mighty power.

R. I will bless your name forever, Lord.

The eyes of all look hopefully to you, and you give them their food in due season; with open hand you satisfy the living according to their need.

R. I will bless your name forever, Lord.

My mouth will speak in praise of the Lord; let every creature bless his holy name, for ever and ever. Amen.

R. I will bless your name forever, Lord.

Colossians 1:15-20

He is the image of the unseen God,
the first born of all creation,
for in him all things were created,
visible and invisible:
whether thrones or dominions or rulers or powers . . .

All was made through him and for him.
He himself is before all things,
and in him all things hold together.
He is the head of the body, the Church;
he is the beginning, the first to be raised from the dead,
so that he might come to have first place in everything.

For in him all the fullness of God was pleased to dwell,
and through him God was pleased to reconcile all things with himself;
through him, through his blood shed on the cross,
God establishes peace,
on earth as in heaven.

1 John 4:16

R. Alleluia, alleluia, alleluia.
God is love. Whoever lives in love, lives in God and God in him.

R. Alleluia, alleluia, alleluia.

So when he saw the crowds, Jesus went up the mountain and sat down. His disciples gathered round, and he began to teach them. This is what he said:

"Blessed are those who know they are needy;
theirs is the kingdom of God.

Blessed are those who suffer grief;
for they shall be comforted.

Blessed are the gentle-hearted;
for they shall inherit the land.

Blessed are those who hunger and thirst to do
what is right;
for they shall be satisfied.

Blessed are the merciful;
for they shall obtain mercy.

Blessed are those who work for peace;
for they shall be called God's children.

Blessed are those who suffer for doing what is
right;
for theirs is the kingdom of God.

And blessed are you, if ever people insult you
or persecute you or slander you on my
account.

Be glad and rejoice, for a great reward awaits you
from God.

That, too, was how they treated the Prophets
before you."

Prayer

Thank you God for this new day in my life. This is a day that will never return again, a day that will have as much meaning as I choose to give to it. Much will depend upon my attitude towards what is happening to me. By giving me this day, Lord, you are giving me time to deepen my relationship with you, time to get my priorities straight, time to grieve, time to laugh, time to hope. In some way, my confinement reminds me of how much my tomorrow will be shaped by how I handle myself today in the midst of crisis and opportunity. So be with me, Lord, and help me to make good use of my time by treasuring the blessings you bestow on me this day. Thank you for this time to give and to receive, to be silent and to speak, to hold on and to let go, to be involved and to withdraw, to reflect and most of all to pray. Let me never forget, Lord, that in your eyes a day is like a thousand years, and a thousand years is like a day. Help me to keep things in perspective. Amen.

2. GOD'S HEART GOES OUT TO US WHEN WE SUFFER OR ARE IN NEED

Isaiah 61:1-3a

The Spirit of the Lord God is upon me,
    because He has anointed me to bring good
    news to the poor.
He has sent me to bind up broken hearts,
    to proclaim liberty to the captives, and free-
    dom to those in prison;
to announce a year of favor from God and a day
    of vengeance from the Lord;
to give solace to those who grieve;

to comfort those who mourn in Zion and
to give them a garland instead of ashes,
oil of gladness instead of lamentation,
a garment of praise, not a mantle of despair.

Ps 25:6-7, 17-18, 20-21

R. To you, O Lord, I lift up my soul.

Be mindful of your mercy, Lord, and of your steadfast love from of old. Remember not the sins of my youth, my rebellious ways and my transgressions, but in your steadfast love, remember me.

R. To you, O Lord, I lift up my soul.

Relieve the troubles of my heart, and free me from my distress. Put an end to my suffering and affliction, and forgive me all my sins.

R. To you, O Lord, I lift up my soul.

Guard my life and deliver me. Let me not be put to shame. It is in you that I take refuge. Let integrity and uprightness preserve me, for all my hope lies, O Lord, in you.

R. To you, O Lord, I lift up my soul.

1 Corinthians 12:12-14, 26-27

As the body is one, though it has many members, and all the members, while being many, form one body, so it is with Christ. All of us, whether Jews or Greeks, slaves or free, have been baptized in one Spirit to form one body and all of us have been given to drink from the one Spirit. The body is not one member, but many.... When one member suffers, all suffer, and when one member is honored, all rejoice. Now you are the body of Christ and each of you individually is a member of it.

1 Corinthians 12:18

> R. Alleluia, alleluia, alleluia.
>
> God arranged the members in the body, each one of them as he chose.
>
> R. Alleluia, alleluia, alleluia.

Mark 8:1-10a

During this period, when a large multitude had again come together and had nothing to eat, Jesus summoned his disciples and said to them, "My heart goes out to these people; they have been with me now for three days and have nothing to eat. If I let them go home hungry, they will faint on the way, and there are some who have come a great distance." "But this place is a desert," his disciples replied. "What hope is there of getting bread out here to feed this crowd?" "How many loaves do you have?" he asked. And they said, "Seven." Then he told the people to sit on the ground. He took the seven loaves and gave thanks; then, breaking them, he gave them to the disciples to serve to the people. This they did. They also had a few small fish. Jesus said grace over them and told the disciples to serve these as well. When everyone had eaten and was satisfied, they gathered up the scraps that remained, twelve baskets full. Now there were about four thousand people. Jesus dismissed them and then embarked in the boat with his disciples.

Merciful Jesus, you were sent to bring solace to the sorrowing. As I thank you for your compassion and concern, I'm reminded of another aspect of your healing ministry, one that directly involves each one of us. You have asked us to share your cross, and have given us a mission which calls us away from self-pity to a proclamation of your Good News even in the midst of tears. You were a wounded healer and have invited us to be the same. Bind up our wounds and strengthen us for the task ahead. Give us the serenity and faith we need to reach out to others with your love. Keep us always in your peace. I ask this in your most holy name. Amen.

3. GOD CONSOLES US IN OUR GRIEF

Wisdom 4:7-14, 15b

The just, even if they die before their time, will be at rest. Old age is not honored because of the length of one's days, nor is the number of years a true measure of one's life. Understanding is one's gray hair and a spotless life, a ripe old age. There were some who pleased God and were loved by him, and while living among sinners were taken up. God removed them so that evil might not impair their understanding or deceit beguile their souls. For the fascination of what is wicked often obscures what is good, and restless desires pervert the innocent heart. Being perfected in a short time, they fulfilled long years, for their souls were pleasing to the Lord. Therefore, he took them quickly from the midst of wickedness. God's grace and mercy are with his elect; he watches over his holy ones.

Psalm 103:8, 10, 13-14, 15-16, 17-18

R. The Lord is kind and merciful.

Gracious and merciful is the Lord, abounding in love and slow to anger. He does not deal with us according to our sins or punish us as we deserve.

R. The Lord is kind and merciful.

As a father has compassion on his children, so the Lord has compassion on those who fear him. For he knows how we were formed; he remembers that we are dust.

R. The Lord is kind and merciful.

Our mortal days are like grass; we bloom like a flower in the fields. The wind passes and we are gone, never to be seen there again.

R. The Lord is kind and merciful.

But the steadfast love of the Lord for those who fear him is everlasting, as is his justice for their children's offspring, for those who keep his covenant and remember to obey his commandments.

R. The Lord is kind and merciful.

Revelation 21:1-5a

Then I saw a new heaven and a new earth. The first heaven and the first earth had passed away and no longer was there sea. I saw the new Jerusalem, the holy city, coming down out of heaven from God prepared as a bride adorned for her husband. A loud voice came from the throne saying, "Here is the dwelling place of God among men. He will dwell with them as their God; and they will be his people. God will be with them; he will wipe every tear from their eyes. There shall be no more death or mourning, crying out or pain, for the world that was has passed away." The One seated on the throne said, "See, I make all things new."

John 11:25

R. Alleluia, alleluia, alleluia.

I am the resurrection and the life, said the Lord: he who believes in me will not die forever.

R. Alleluia, alleluia, alleluia.

John 11:20-30, 32-45

When Martha heard that Jesus was coming, she went to meet him while Mary stayed at home. And she said to Jesus, "Lord, if you had been here, my brother would not have died. Still I know that whatever you ask from God, God will give you." Jesus said, "Your brother will rise again." Martha replied, "I know that he will rise again in the resurrection of the dead on the last day." Jesus said to her, "I am the resurrection and the life. Those who believe in me, even though they die, will live, and everyone who lives and believes in me will never die. Do you believe this?" She said to him, "Yes, Lord, I believe that you are the Messiah, the Son of God, the One who is coming into the world." After that, Martha went and called her sister Mary, quietly, saying, "The Master is here and is asking for you." As soon as Mary heard this, she rose and went to him. When she came to the place where Jesus was and saw him, she fell at his feet and said, "Lord, if you had been here, my brother would not have died." When Jesus saw her weeping and the Jews also who had come with her, he was greatly disturbed in spirit and deeply moved. He said, "Where have you laid him?" And they answered, "Lord, come and see." And Jesus wept. The Jews said, "See how he loved him!" Deeply moved again, Jesus drew near to the tomb. It was a cave with a stone laid across it. Jesus ordered, "Take the stone away." Martha said to him, "Lord, there will be a stench for he has been dead four days." Jesus replied, "Did I not tell you that if you believed, you would see the glory of God?" So they took away the stone. And Jesus lifted up his eyes and said, "Father, I thank you for having heard me. I knew that you always hear me, but I have said this for the sake of these people standing here, so that they may believe that you sent me." When he had said this, he cried out in a loud voice, "Lazarus, come out!" The dead man came out, his hands and feet bound with linen strips and his face wrapped in a cloth. Jesus said to them, "Unbind him and let him go." Many of the Jews therefore, who had come with Mary and had seen what Jesus did, believed in him.

Prayer

Lord, you never promised to take away our darkness or the struggle of our every day. Rather you promised to be our light in time of darkness and our strength in time of need. Help us not to be blind to your light or insensitive to your presence as we grieve the loss of one whom we have loved so much. Give us courage to face the days ahead; grant us peace in our agony and loss; keep our family always united in your name. Grant us the serenity to accept without bitterness that which we cannot change. Give us hope to see beyond today and the faith to accept your will. Help us to always trust your promises. Into your hands and into your care we entrust that precious life which you, in your goodness, have given to us to love and to share. Amen.

4. GOD GIVES US COURAGE IN OUR FEAR

Wisdom 5:14-20

The hope of the godless is like chaff blown in the wind,
like a thin frost melted in the storm,
like smoke dispersed by the wind;
it fades like the memory of a guest who stays but a day.

But the upright live forever,
their reward is with the Lord
and the Most High keeps them in his care.
This is why they will receive a glorious crown
and a beautiful diadem from the hand of the Lord.
He will shelter them with his right hand
and his arm will be their shield.

He will put on justice as his breastplate
and right judgment as his helmet,
invincible holiness will be his shield,
implacable anger will serve as his sword,
and the universe will march with him against his frenzied
foes.

Psalm 27:1, 4, 7, 8, 9, 13-14

R. The Lord is my light and my salvation.

The Lord is my light, my salvation; whom shall I fear? The Lord is my battlement, my defender; of whom shall I be afraid?

R. The Lord is my light and my salvation.

One thing I ask of the Lord, one thing I seek: to dwell in the house of the Lord all the days of my life, to behold the beauty of the Lord and to seek counsel in his sanctuary.

R. The Lord is my light and my salvation.

Hear my voice when I call, O Lord; have mercy on me and answer me. Your presence, O Lord, I seek. Do not hide your face from me.

R. The Lord is my light and my salvation.

I hope to see the goodness of the Lord in the land of the living. Trust in the Lord, be strong and courageous. Yes, wait for the Lord.

R. The Lord is my light and my salvation.

Romans 8:15-17

You did not receive a spirit of slavery to fall back into fear again, but the Spirit that makes you adopted children. Every time we cry, "Abba! Father!", the Spirit assures our spirit that we are children of God. If we are his children, then we are his heirs as well. Ours will be the inheritance of God and we will share it with Christ; for if we suffer now with him, we will also share his Glory.

John 6:39

R. Alleluia, alleluia, alleluia.

This is the will of my Father, says the Lord, that I should lose nothing of all that he has given to me.

R. Alleluia, alleluia, alleluia.

Luke 12:22-32

I tell you, therefore," he said to his disciples, "do not worry over the needs of your life or body — what to eat or what to wear; for life is worth more than that which nourishes it and the body more than clothing. Learn from the crows; they neither sow nor reap, they have neither stores nor barns, but God still looks after them. And you, are you not much more important than they? Can any of you by worrying about it add a single hour to your span of life? And if even that much is not in your power, why are you so anxious about the rest? Look at the lilies; they neither toil nor spin. And yet, I tell you, Solomon in all his glory was not dressed like one of these. If that is how God clothes the grass of the field, which blooms today and tomorrow is thrown into the fire, how much more will he look after you, for all your want of faith! So don't be anxious about what you are to eat and drink. Do not worry about it. Let the people of the world run after these things; your Father knows that you need them. Let your care, rather, be for God's kingdom, and these things will be given to you as well. Do not be afraid, little flock, for it has pleased your Father to give you the kingdom."

God grant me the
> *Serenity* to accept the things I cannot change;
> *Courage* to change the things I can; and
> *Wisdom* to know the difference.

Help me to live one day at a time

Enjoy one moment at a time

Accept hardships as the pathway to peace

Taking, as He did, this sinful world as it is,
> not as I would have it

Trusting that He will make all things right
> if I but surrender to His will

That I may be reasonably happy in this life
> and supremely happy with Him forever in the next.
> Amen.

5. GOD AWAITS US WHEN WE DIE

Wisdom 3:1-6, 9

The souls of the just are in the hands of God and no torment will ever touch them. In the eyes of the foolish, they seemed to have died, and their departure was thought to be a disaster. In their going from us they seemed to have lost everything; but they are in peace. For though in the sight of others they seem to have been punished, their hope is full of immortality. After having been afflicted a little, they shall be greatly blessed, because God has tested them and found them worthy to be with him; like gold in the furnace he tried them, and like a sacrificial offering he accepted them. Those who trust in him will understand the truth. Those who are faithful will abide with him in love, because grace and mercy are with his holy ones, and he watches over his elect.

Psalm 42:2, 3, 5; 43:3, 4, 5

R. My soul is thirsting for the living God. When shall I see him face to face?

As a deer longs for flowing streams, so my soul pines for you, O God.

R. My soul is thirsting for the living God. When shall I see him face to face?

My soul thirsts for God, the living God. When shall I go and see the face of God?

R. My soul is thirsting for the living God. When shall I see him face to face?

These things I remember as I pour out my soul, how I used to lead the faithful in procession to the house of God, amid shouts of joy and thanksgiving, among the feasting throng.

R. My soul is thirsting for the living God. When shall I see him face to face?

Send forth your light and your truth; let them be my guide. Let them take me to your holy mountain, to the place where you reside.

R. My soul is thirsting for the living God. When shall I see him face to face?

Then will I go to the altar of God, to God, my gladness and my delight. Then will I give you thanks upon the harp, O God, my God!

R. My soul is thirsting for the living God. When shall I see him face to face?

Why are you so downcast, O my soul? Why do you sigh within me? Hope in God, for again shall I praise him, my savior and my God.

R. My soul is thirsting for the living God. When shall I see him face to face?

1 Thessalonians 4:13-18

We do not want you to be mistaken, brothers and sisters, about those who have died, lest you grieve as do others who have no hope. For since we believe that Jesus died and rose again, even so will God bring forth with him from the dead those who have also died believing in him. We say this to you as if the Lord himself had said it: those of us who are alive, who are left until the coming of the Lord, will in no way have an advantage over those who have died. For the Lord himself — with a cry of command, with the archangel's voice and God's trumpet — will descend from heaven. Then those who have died in the Lord will rise first. As for those of us who are alive, who are left, we will be caught up with them in the clouds to meet the Lord in the air. And we will be with the Lord forever. Encourage one another with this message.

Philippians 3:20

R. Alleluia, alleluia, alleluia.

Our true home is in heaven, and Jesus, whose return we long for, will come from heaven to save us.

R. Alleluia, alleluia, alleluia.

 18

John 14:1-7

J esus said to his disciples, "Don't let your hearts be troubled. Have faith in God and faith in me. In my Father's house there are many rooms. Were that not so would I have told you that I am going in order to prepare a place for you? And if I go to prepare a place for you, I will come back again and will take you to myself, so that where I am you may also be."

Prayer

O Lord, You are the resurrection and the life. You have promised that whoever believes in You, even if they die, will have a life that never ends. May this sacred promise comfort us in our sadness, that we may take solace in the hope of a life of unending and perfect happiness with you in heaven. Help us to realize that those who die believing in You will live forever. O Savior of the world, reassure us in our belief that life does not end in death, but is merely changed. When we leave this world, we enter a life of perfect joy in your presence and in the presence of a Father who loves us, of the Spirit who sanctifies us, of a Mother who watches over us and of all the saints who have prayed for us. As we commend to your loving care your servant

_____,

whom you have called to yourself, we confidently ask that he/she may enjoy this life with you forever. Grant this in your most holy name. Amen.

6. God rejoices when we repent and is pleased when we give thanks

Zephaniah 3:17-20

The Lord, your God, is in your midst, a warrior who gives victory. He will rejoice over you with gladness and will renew you in his love. He will exult over you with loud singing as on a day of festival. "I will remove the threat of doom from you, so that none may recount your disgrace. I will deal with all your oppressors at that time. And I will rescue all the lame and bring the exiles home. I will change their shame into honor and they will be renowned in all the earth. The time is coming when I will bring your scattered people home. I will make you famous and praised throughout the world when I bring about your restoration before your very eyes," says the Lord.

Psalm 96:1-2, 2-3, 7-8, 10

R. Proclaim his marvelous deeds to all the nations.

Sing to the Lord a new song, sing to the Lord, all the earth! Sing to the Lord and praise his name.

R. Proclaim his marvelous deeds to all the nations.

Tell of his salvation day after day. Declare his glory among the nations, his wonderful deeds among all peoples.

R. Proclaim his marvelous deeds to all the nations.

Give to the Lord, O families of nations, give to the Lord glory and praise. Give to the Lord the glory due his name.

R. Proclaim his marvelous deeds to all the nations.

Say among the nations, "The Lord is king!" The world he made is firmly established and shall never be moved. With justice he governs his people.

R. Proclaim his marvelous deeds to all the nations.

1 Peter 1:3-9

Let us praise God, the Father of our Lord Jesus Christ, for by his great mercy he has given us a new birth into a living hope through the resurrection of Jesus Christ from the dead, and into an inheritance that is imperishable, undefiled and unfading. This inheritance is kept in heaven for you who, through faith, are being protected by the power of God until your salvation which stands ready to be revealed in the last days. Be glad about this even though for a while you may have to suffer many trials so that the genuineness of your faith — more precious than gold that is perishable even though tested by fire — may prove to result in praise and glory and honor when Jesus Christ appears. Although you have not seen him, you love him; and even though you do not see him now, you still believe in him and rejoice with an indescribable joy tinged with glory, for you are attaining the goal of your faith: the salvation of your souls.

2 Corinthians 6:16

R. Alleluia, alleluia, alleluia.

My dwelling place shall be with them, says the Lord. I will be their God and they will be my people.

R. Alleluia, alleluia, alleluia.

Luke 15:1-7

Now tax collectors and social outcasts were seeking the company of Jesus, all of them eager to hear what he had to say. But the Pharisees and doctors of the law frowned at this, muttering, "This man welcomes sinners and eats with them." So Jesus told them the following story: "Suppose one of you has a hundred sheep and loses one of them. Will he not leave the ninety-nine on the moor and go looking for the one that was lost until he finds it? And finding it, will he not joyfully carry it back on his shoulders? Then he will call his friends and neighbors together, saying, 'Rejoice with me, for I have found my lost sheep.' Just so, I tell you, there will be more rejoicing in heaven over one repentant sinner than over ninety-nine upright who have no need to repent."

— or —

Luke 17:11-17

On his way to Jerusalem, Jesus was passing through the region between Samaria and Galilee. As he was entering a certain village, ten lepers approached him. Keeping their distance, they called out to him, "Jesus, Master, have pity on us!" Noticing them, Jesus said to them, "Go and show yourselves to the priests." Now, as they went their way, they found that they were cured. One of them, realizing that he had been cleansed, turned back, praising God in a loud voice. Throwing himself at the feet of Jesus, he thanked him. This man was a Samaritan. "Were not the ten made clean?" Jesus asked. "Where, then, are the other nine? Was none of them willing to come back and give thanks to God but this foreigner?" Then Jesus said to him, "Get up and go on your way; your faith has made you well."

Prayer

God our Father, you have fashioned us in your own image and likeness, persons who are beautiful and precious in your sight but also fragile and weak. In the face of my sins and imperfections make me aware not only of what is wrong but also of what is right with me. In my confinement let me not forget that I still have my eyes to contemplate the beauty of your creation, to appreciate the sunrise and the sunset, trees and flowers, color and light. Help me to see your image reflected in the faces of your people. Don't let me wait until I meet the blind to appreciate this blessing! I still have my ears to hear the song bird in its flight, the gentle sound of rain, the voices of those I love. Don't let me wait until I meet the deaf to value this! I still have my hands to reach out to those in need, to touch and to embrace. O Lord, may I never forget that I am the fragile but sacred temple of your presence and may I forever thank you that I am, by you, so marvelously, wonderfully kept. Amen.

Sirach 51:1-12

I give you thanks, O Lord and King; I praise you, God my Savior. I give thanks to your name, for you are my help and my protector. You delivered my body from destruction, from the snare of the wicked tongue and from lips that speak but lies. In the presence of my adversaries you were my helper, my deliverer, in the fullness of your mercy and the greatness of your name. From grinding teeth about to devour me, from the hand of those seeking my life, from the many troubles I endured, you saved me. You rescued me from choking fire on every side and from the midst of fire that I had not kindled. From the depths of the netherworld, from an impure tongue and lying word, from vicious slander reported to the king, you delivered me. My soul drew near to death, and my life was on the brink of the world below. I was surrounded on every side and there was no one to help me; I looked for human assistance and there was none. Then I remembered your mercy, O Lord, and your kindness from of old. For you rescue those who wait for you and save them from their enemies. So I sent up my prayer from the earth, and begged for deliverance from death. I cried out, "Lord, you are my Father; do not forsake me in the day of trouble, when there is no help against the proud. I will praise your name continually, and will sing you hymns of thanksgiving." My prayer was heard, for you saved me from destruction and rescued me in time of trouble.

For this reason I thank and praise you, and I bless the name of the Lord.

R. Into your hands, O Lord, I entrust my spirit.

Be a rock for my refuge, a stronghold for my safety. My rock and my fortress, lead me for your name's sake and guide me in your way.

R. Into your hands, O Lord, I entrust my spirit.

Into your hands I commend my spirit; you have redeemed me, O Lord, O faithful God. I put all my trust in the Lord; I will rejoice and be glad in your love.

R. Into your hands, O Lord, I entrust my spirit.

Be merciful to me, O Lord, in my affliction; my eyes have grown dim with sorrow, my body emaciated and my soul weak. But I put my trust in you, O Lord for you are my God.

R. Into your hands, O Lord, I entrust my spirit.

Make your face shine upon your servant; save me in your love. Be strong and take courage, all you whose hope is in the Lord.

R. Into your hands, O Lord, I entrust my spirit.

Romans 8:31-35, 37-39

What then are we to say about these things? If God is for us, who can be against us? He who did not withhold his own Son, but gave him up for all of us, will he not with him also give us everything else? Who will bring any charge against God's elect?

It is God who justifies. Who is to condemn? Will it be Christ Jesus, who died, and still more rose and is seated at the right hand of God interceding for us? Who will separate us from the love of Christ? Will hardship, or distress, or persecution, or famine, or nakedness, or peril, or the sword? No, in all these things we are more than conquerors through him who loved us. I am convinced that neither death, nor life, nor angels, nor rulers, nor things present nor things to come, nor powers, nor height, nor depth, nor anything else in all creation will be able to separate us from the love of God which we have in Christ Jesus our Lord.

James 1:12

>R. Alleluia, alleluia, alleluia.

>Happy are those who stand firm when trials come; they have proved themselves and will win the crown of life.

>R. Alleluia, alleluia, alleluia.

Mark 6:45-56

Jesus made the disciples embark in the boat and go across to Bethsaida ahead of him, while he himself sent the crowd away. Then after seeing them off, he went up into the hills to pray. As night fell, the boat was in the middle of the lake while Jesus was alone on the land. He could see them laboring at the oars, for the wind was against them, so he came towards them about three in the morning, walking on the lake. He was going to pass them by, but when they saw him walking on the water, they thought it was a ghost and cried out. They had all seen him and were terrified. He immediately called out to them, "Take heart. It is I. Do not be afraid." Then he climbed into the boat with them and the wind died down. They were completely dumbfounded, for they had not learned the lesson of the loaves; their minds were still closed. Having crossed the lake, they came ashore at Gennesaret where they tied up the boat. As soon as they had landed, people recognized Jesus and ran to spread the news throughout the countryside. Wherever he was they brought to him the sick lying on their mats. And everywhere he went, to villages, towns or farms, they laid the sick in the marketplace and begged him to let them touch just the fringe of his cloak. All who touched him were made well.

Prayer

O Lord, I am so nervous and anxious in this place. I've never liked to be confined and have always prized my freedom. Those who are in here with me only remind me of my isolation. But here I am, determined to take care of myself as best I can. I am not at ease in these surroundings, too many professionals and too many people who seem to know more about me than I know about myself. I have all kinds of questions which I'm afraid to ask — partly because I don't want to look naive or ignorant, but partly because I don't want to hear the answers. Everyone seems so busy, too. I feel they don't have time for me. At times I get so nervous I wish I could run away. That's the way I am sometimes — a nervous wreck. Lord, help me to cool it and to relax a bit. Help me to laugh at myself and at my worries. Help me to surrender to your will and my fate. Give me a mature, positive and trusting attitude in this time of stress. Let me hear your words, "Be not afraid for I am with you." I ask this in your most holy name. Amen.

8. GOD GIVES US HOPE IN TIME OF TROUBLE

Lamentations 3:17-26

Of peace he has deprived my soul, I have forgotten what happiness is; so I say, "Gone are my hopes, and all that I had hoped for from the Lord." The thought of my affliction and my homelessness is so much wormwood and gall! Thinking it over and over, my soul is downcast and humbled. But this is what I call to mind and therefore I have hope. The steadfast love of the Lord never ceases, his mercies never end; they are new every morning; his love is ever faithful. "The Lord is my portion," says my soul, "therefore I will hope in him." The Lord is good to those who wait for him, to the soul that seeks him.

Psalm 23:1-3, 3-4, 5, 6

R. The Lord is my shepherd; there is nothing I shall want.

The Lord is my shepherd, I shall not want. He makes me lie down in green pastures. Beside restful waters he leads me; he refreshes my soul.

R. The Lord is my shepherd; there is nothing I shall want.

He leads me in right paths for his name's sake. Even though I walk through the valley of darkness, I fear no evil; for you are with me. Your rod and your staff are there to reassure me.

R. The Lord is my shepherd; there is nothing I shall want.

You prepare a table before me in the presence of my foes. You anoint my head with oil; my cup overflows.

R. The Lord is my shepherd; there is nothing I shall want.

Only goodness and kindness shall follow me all the days of my life, and I shall dwell in the house of the Lord as long as I live.

R. The Lord is my shepherd; there is nothing I shall want.

2 Corinthians 5:1, 6-10

We know that if this earthly tent we live in is destroyed, we may count on a heavenly dwelling, a building built by God, not made with hands, eternal in the heavens. So we are always confident. We know that while we dwell in the body, we are away from the Lord. We walk by faith, not by sight. Indeed, we are so confident that we would rather be away from the body to go to live with the Lord. So whether we are with him or away, we make it our aim to please him, for we all have to appear before the judgment seat of Christ that each may receive what he or she deserves for the good or evil deeds done in the present life.

Matthew 25:34

R. Alleluia, alleluia, alleluia.

Come, you whom my Father has blessed, says the Lord; inherit the kingdom prepared for you since the foundation of the world.

R. Alleluia, alleluia, alleluia.

Luke 11:5-13

He said to them, "Suppose one of you has a friend, and you go to him in the middle of the night and say, 'Friend, lend me three loaves. A friend of mine is on a journey and has stopped to spend the night with me, and I have nothing to offer him.' Suppose this man shouts in answer from inside, 'Don't bother me at this hour! I've locked the door and the children and I are in bed. I can't get up to give you bread.' I tell you, even though this man might not get up to attend to him because he is his friend, he will get up because of the other's persistence. And he will give him all he needs. So I say to you, Ask and you will receive, seek and you will find, knock and the door will be opened to you. Everyone who asks receives; everyone who seeks finds; everyone who knocks has the door opened to him. If a son asks for a fish, will any father among you give him a serpent? If he asks for an egg, will you give him a scorpion? If even you, sinners though you be, know how to give good gifts to your children, how much more will the Father in heaven give the Holy Spirit to those who ask him?"

O Lord, help me believe that behind the clouds there is the sun even when it rains, help me believe the barren trees of autumn will bear new leaves again if I am patient enough to wait. Help me to realize that the only way to reach a mountain is through deep valleys and rugged climbs, that the only way a candle can share its light is through its consummation. Teach me to let go of the securities that make me insecure and to let go of the fears that make me irritable and impatient. I do not like to ask for help in time of trouble. I've always prided myself on my self-sufficiency and independence. And still I am your child. Remind me that we must ask if we're to receive, to seek if we're to find, to knock if we're to gain access to your grace. Help me to trust what I cannot control, to walk where I cannot see, to believe that behind the lowering clouds there is your rising sun. Amen.

9. GOD RESTORES US TO HEALTH IN BODY, MIND AND SOUL

Ezekiel 34:11-16, 25b-27

Indeed the Lord God says this: I myself will care for my sheep and watch over them. As the shepherd looks after his flock when he finds them scattered, so will I watch over my sheep and gather them from all the places to which they have wandered on a day of dark clouds and dense fog. I will bring them out from the nations and gather them from other lands. I will lead them into their own land and will feed them on the mountains of Israel and in all the rich valleys and inhabited regions of the land. I will take them to good pastures on the high mountains of Israel. They will rest where the grazing is good and feed in lush meadows on the heights of Israel. I myself will tend my sheep and let them rest. I will seek the lost and bring back the strayed. I will bind up the injured and strengthen the weak. I will rid the land of wild beasts so that they may live safely in the desert and sleep in the forests. I will settle them on my holy mountain, sending them rain in season, showers of rich blessings. The trees of the field will give their fruit and the soil its produce, while they are safe in their land. And they will know that I am their God.

Isaiah 38:10, 11, 12, 14b, 16

R. You have saved my life, O Lord; I shall not die.

Once I said: In the noontide of my life I must depart; I am consigned to the land of the dead for the rest of my years.

R. You have saved my life, O Lord; I shall not die.

I said, I shall not see the Lord again in the land of the living; never again shall I look on my brothers and sisters among those who inhabit the earth.

R. You have saved my life, O Lord; I shall not die.

Like a shepherd's tent, my dwelling has been torn down and borne away; like a weaver, you have rolled up my life and cut it from the loom.

R. You have saved my life, O Lord; I shall not die.

Come and help me, Lord, for I am troubled! Those live whom the Lord protects. Yours alone is . . . the life of my spirit. Restore me to health and make me live.

R. You have saved my life, O Lord; I shall not die.

James 5:13-16

Are there any among you who are suffering? Let them pray. Are any cheerful? Let them sing songs of praise. Are any among you sick? Let them call for the elders of the Church who shall pray over them, anointing them with oil in the name of the Lord. The prayer of faith will save the sick, and the Lord will raise them up, and any who have sinned will be forgiven.

Mathew 8:17

R. Alleluia, alleluia, alleluia.

He took our sicknesses away; he carried our infirmities for us.

R. Alleluia, alleluia, alleluia.

Matthew 15:29-31

Jesus then left that country and came to the Sea of Galilee. There he climbed the mountain where he seated himself. Great crowds came to him, bringing with them the lame, the maimed, the blind, the mute and many others who were suffering. The people carried them to the feet of Jesus, and he healed them. All were amazed when they saw the mute speaking, the maimed made whole, the lame walking and the blind able to see. And they praised the God of Israel.

Prayer

God, our Father, you are the source of strength and hope. Bless this place where I find myself that it may be not only a place of sickness and suffering but also a place of healing and caring. Bless the people whom you have chosen to be the instruments of your healing, that they may be humble and knowledgeable channels of your grace. Where there is danger may they protect life; where there is weakness and pain may they provide relief and comfort; where there is anxiety and fear may they offer gentle reassurance through their presence; and where all human efforts fail may they rest reassured that we can rest secure with you. Bless all your workers, Lord, with a gentle and compassionate heart for this is how they will find the door to people's hearts and concerns. Bless me, too, so that through this experience I may strengthen my faith in you and be granted health of body, mind and soul. I ask this in Jesus' name. Amen.

10. God answers us when we pray

Esther C:13:8-10, 15-17

Recalling all that the Lord had done, Mordecai prayed to him and said: "O Lord God, almighty King, all things are in your power, and no one can withstand you in your will to save Israel. You made heaven and earth and every wonderful thing under the heavens. You are the Lord of all, and no one can resist you, Lord. And now, Lord, God and King, God of Abraham, spare your people, for our enemies plan our ruin and are bent upon destroying the inheritance that was yours from the beginning. Do not forsake your portion, which you redeemed for yourself out of Egypt. Hear my prayer; have mercy on your inheritance and turn our sorrow into joy: thus we shall live to sing praise to your name, O Lord. Do not silence the lips of those who praise you."

Psalm 89:2-3, 4-5, 21-22, 25, 27

R. Forever will I sing the goodness of the Lord.

I will sing forever, Lord, of your steadfast love; your faithfulness I will proclaim from age to age. I will declare how lasting is your love, how firm your faithfulness in heaven.

R. Forever will I sing the goodness of the Lord.

You said, "I have made a covenant with my chosen one, I have sworn to my servant David: 'Forever will I establish your descendants and preserve your throne for all generations.'"

R. Forever will I sing the goodness of the Lord.

"I have found my servant David; and with my holy oil I have anointed him. My hand shall remain with him always, and my arm shall make him strong."

R. Forever will I sing the goodness of the Lord.

"My faithful, steadfast love will be with him; and through my name his horn will be exalted. He shall say to me, 'You are my Father, my God, my Rock, my Savior.'"

R. Forever will I sing the goodness of the Lord.

Hebrews 4:14-16; 5:7-9

We have a great High Priest who has entered heaven, Jesus, the Son of God. Let us, then, hold fast to the faith that we profess. Our high priest is not indifferent to our weaknesses, for he was tempted in every way that we are, yet without sinning. Let us therefore approach the throne of grace with confidence that we may receive mercy and find grace to help us in our time of need. In the days of his mortal life, Christ offered up prayers and supplications with loud cries and tears to the one who was able to save him from death. And he was heard because of his reverent submission. Although he was [God's] Son, he learned obedience through what he suffered and, having been made perfect, he became the source of eternal salvation for all who obey him.

John 15:7

> R. Alleluia, alleluia, alleluia.
> "If you live in me, and my words stay part of you, you may ask what you will and it will be done for you."
> R. Alleluia, alleluia, alleluia.

Luke 18:1-8

To show how one must pray always without losing heart, Jesus told this parable: "In a certain town there was a judge who feared neither God nor had respect for others. And in the same town there was a widow who kept coming to him saying, `Grant me justice against my opponent.' For a time he refused, but eventually he said to himself, `I have no fear of God or respect for anyone, but this woman is getting on my nerves. I will see to it that she gets justice; then perhaps she'll stop badgering me with her continual coming.'" And the Lord said, "Just listen to what the unjust judge is saying. Will not God grant justice to his chosen ones who cry out to him day and night? Will he delay long in helping them? I tell you, he will speedily grant them justice."

Prayer

God of mercy, look kindly on us in our suffering. Ease our burden and make our faith strong that we may always have confidence and trust in your fatherly care. Be our strength in adversity, our health in weakness and our comfort in sorrow. Teach us to acknowledge always the many good things your infinite love has given us and grant us your pardon and your peace. We know that you hear our prayers and answer them when we ask with faith and according to your most holy will through Christ our Lord. Amen.

PART TWO: MISCELLANEOUS POEMS AND PRAYERS

1. LOVELY LADY DRESSED IN BLUE

Lovely Lady dressed in blue —
Teach me how to pray!
God was just your little Boy,
Tell me what to say!
Did you lift Him up, sometimes,
Gently, on your knee?
Did you sing to Him the way
Mother does to me?
Did you hold His hand at night?
Did you ever try
Telling stories of the world?
O! And did He cry?
Do you really think He cares
If I tell Him things —
Little things that happen? And
Do the Angels' wings
Make a noise? And can He hear
Me if I speak low?
Does He understand me now?
Tell me for you know!
Lovely Lady dressed in blue,
Teach me how to pray!
God was just your little Boy,
And you know the way.

— Mary Dixon Thayer

2. Prayer for a Newborn Baby

O Lord, you are the giver of all life, human and divine. You came into this world as a little child in order that we might have life and have it to the full. We are grateful for the life you have given us and for making us bearers of life to others, too. We rejoice in the miracle of the new life that has been born into our midst and for choosing us as instruments of this new creation. As you have given us the joy of being life-givers, help us to be life-sustainers by sharing our love and care with this little baby who is already a cherished part of our growing family. Send your Holy Spirit to protect and guide our child throughout his/her life. We ask this in your most holy name. Amen.

3. Prayer for a Dying Child

O Lord, words are so hard to find. There is so much we don't understand, so much that is upsetting us. We have tears in our eyes and pain in our hearts as the story of a promising beginning has already turned into a tale that is about to end. We asked for so little and we were hit with so much. We dreamed and waited in vain. Now we're left with a sadness and an emptiness that no treasure in the world can fill. Help us, Lord, to realize that our child will always be a part of our life as he/she was a part of our dreams. Help us to accept, too — at times through the fault of no one — that life is too fragile to be sustained and we need to accept what we cannot change. Take care of our baby, Lord. Give him/her a special place in your kingdom and help us to find strength in the light you offer us. We ask this in Jesus' name. Amen.

4. Angel in Disguise

Two graven dates, a bas-relief
of cherubs mark a life as brief
as lightning on that April day.

A fault at birth, no matter whose,
provoked the struggle he would lose
as autumn staged her last display.

His parents watched their summer dreams
grow wintry as the doctors' schemes
all ended with advice to pray.

Above the mossy stone each spring
two graying heads incline to bring
to life a memory and say:

We thank Thee, Lord, for in Thy care
an angel taught us how to share
and saved us from our selfish way.

Prince of Peace, bend down to us who seek serenity among the frustrations of daily life. Whisper the Father's will so that we may follow your example of trust and self-giving, and thus attain the quiet acceptance which you offered to all in need. Amen.

— *Roger A. Swenson* in *The Lamp of Life Renewed*

5. Prayer Before Surgery

O Lord, the hours seem so long as they go by. I'm so restless and there are so many thoughts going through my mind, thoughts about the outcome of my surgery, about my future, about my family. I'm afraid and anxious because it's my own body, my own life that's on the line. I raise my voice to you, Lord, so that you may replace my fear with trust and my anxiety with faith in your healing human instruments. Bless the doctors who will perform the surgery. Guide their hands to bring healing where there is sickness, strength where I am weak. Bless my family, too, who through their presence and support have given me the courage I need to face this moment. Bless my night. Help me to rest peacefully under your protection so that I'll be ready for my important day tomorrow. Amen.

6. Prayer of a Cancer Patient

O Lord, I've turned my eyes and prayers to you so very often. There have been times when I've felt forgotten by you and I really wondered if you were still there to hear me. There were times when I got so discouraged that I prayed to die. And other times when I was so sick and so depressed that I couldn't speak to anyone. There were times when I was so angry that I felt like screaming and crying at the same time. And times when I felt so helpless and so hopeless that I didn't even want to try. How often I have hoped and bargained and prayed. Lord, as you hear my cry and see my tears, grant me that peace of mind which comes from trust in you. Help me to live one day at a time, to find new strength in you as my body weakens, to be grateful for all that is done to take away the pain and make me comfortable. Stay by my side as I walk through this dark valley. See me safely to the other side. I ask this in Jesus' name. Amen.

7. Prayer of a Heart Patient

O Lord, it was something that happened all of a sudden. I began feeling chest pains and was really scared there for a while. For a moment there I felt as though I had the whole world on my chest. I'm all right now. In fact, I feel like walking home. But I know I'll have to stay around for a while. I've been so active that I find it hard to just lie here. They tell me I'll have to take it easy now. I've always been so healthy and never thought that I could get sick like this. I'm worried about my family, those who depend on me. I'm concerned about my job and what the future holds in store. Calm my anxieties and quiet my fears. Help me to accept my limitations and to appreciate each day that I live. Give me the grace to see life as a child does, not as a problem to be solved but as a mystery to be discovered with each new day. I ask this in Jesus' name. Amen.

8. Prayer of Someone Who Is Paralyzed

O God, there is so little I can do, so little that I can hope for. Today I wasn't even able to turn my head to watch TV, so they had to move my bed around. I feel so different from others and so dependent on them. I know they can't understand what I'm going through. It's so frustrating and humiliating to be so helpless. And still I feel that I've grown to be a deeper person through my affliction. The disappointments and failures of my body have helped me to discover my inner strength, the treasure of simple gestures, of real gifts. It's not easy to see nurses, people of my own age, walk in and out of my room. I envy them their freedom and wish that they could realize how fortunate they are. I don't look for pity. If my presence here can soften hearts and make them more compassionate then I can believe that there is a purpose in all of this. Help me, Lord, to cope. Amen.

9. Prayer for the Dying

Depart from this world, O Christian soul, in the name of God the Father almighty, who created you; in the name of Jesus Christ, the Son of the living God, who suffered for you; in the name of the Holy Spirit, who has been poured forth upon you; in the name of the holy Mother of God, the Virgin Mary; and in the name of St. Joseph, her illustrious spouse. May peace be your dwelling today, and may your home be in heaven with God. May the Lord who was crucified for your sake, free you from excruciating pain. May he who died for you free you from the death that never ends. May the Son of the living God set you in the ever verdant loveliness of his paradise, and may he, the true Shepherd of our souls, recognize you as one of his very own. May he free you from all your sins and assign you a place at his right hand in the company of his elect in heaven. May you see your Redeemer face to face and, standing in his presence forever, may you behold with joyful eyes your Maker and Savior in all his glory. Then, having taken your place in the ranks of the Blessed in heaven, may you enjoy the happiness of paradise forever. Amen.

10. Prayer for the Dead

God our Father, we are gathered here to say farewell to one whom we have loved, someone who has had a very special place in our hearts and in our lives. We thank you Lord for the times you have given us to share together your gift of love. We pray for your pardon and forgiveness for anything we might have done to hurt each other. Help us, Lord, to live peacefully with the imperfections of our human relationships knowing that you accept us as we are. Comfort us through the memories our loved one leaves with us. May they give us courage in our journey into the future. Grant your servant a place of peace in your kingdom, where there is no more suffering, or crying out, or pain. Bless the one we loved in life and keep him/her in your care. We ask this in the name of the Father and of the Son and of the Holy Spirit. Amen.

INDEX